THREE PEOPLE YOU NEED IN YOUR LIFE

THE PUSHER • THE COACH • THE INSTRUCTOR

PASTOR ANTHONY VANDYKE

PRIMIX
PUBLISHING
THE WRITE CHOICE

Primix Publishing
11620 Wilshire Blvd
Suite 900, West Wilshire Center, Los Angeles, CA, 90025
www.primixpublishing.com
Phone: 1-800-538-5788

Published by Primix Publishing: 02/21/2024

ISBN: 979-8-89194-123-6(sc)
ISBN: 979-8-89194-124-3(e)

CONTENTS

THE INTRODUCTION

The journey to success has everything to do with the people you have in your life.

You are the product of your environment, no matter what you think, your elevation in life greatly depends on those who touch you.

Proverbs 27:17 NASB
As iron sharpens iron,
So one person sharpens another.

Who is your greatest influence?

_____

_____

_____

Why do you consider them your greatest influence?

_____

_____

_____

When I say touch, I really mean those who have a direct influence on the way you think and perceive things. As a pastor, teacher, mentor and business professional I meet people from all walks of life who want to do better.

They really want more from life, but they are stuck in a vicious cycle of wishing and hoping that life would get better for them. Unfortunately, wishing and hoping feels good but it produces little results.

Before we dig deep into the three people you need in your life, please answer the questions below.

What do you want in life?

_____

_____

_____

Who do you know that has what you want in life?

_____

_____

_____

What are the things that you think hold you back in life?

_____

_____

_____

Warning. What I am about to teach you in this manual will contradict all the brainwashing you have attained throughout your life about how to be successful.

To be point blank, most are trained in poverty. Seldom do people elevate beyond those who love them most, it doesn't make them bad people, they are just uninformed. I am not talking bad or down on your parents, auntie, cousin or other precious people in your life. But the old saying is so correct, "The apple doesn't fall far from the tree."

What does your tree look like? If you are not careful, your destiny will look like the tree that produced you.

The journey to greatness starts right now. Are you ready?

Greatness must be desired. You will not climb to the zenith of your career by being passive or using the excuse what God has for me is for me.

Please know, that is absolute nonsense!!

This journey will require you to put in some hard work and change the people in your life immediately.

Changing the people in your life will be the hardest thing you will ever do.

As I am writing this manual, I buried my wife of 28 years and 6 months less than a week ago.

Nicole was all three people to me at different times in our marriage, pusher, coach and instructor. I was very fortunate to have that kind of person in my life. Watch this, at some point I was all three people for her. We were the perfect couple. When I say perfect, we had flaws but our drive and determination is without question. I remember when Nikki told me I was underperforming financially. That was like a kick in the midsection. My ego was bruised and nearly destroyed.

I have discovered most men are insecure and not ready for the truth.

Back to me, I became upset with her. It took me three weeks to gather myself.

After I put on my big boy pants, I discovered she was absolutely correct. I let life's ups and down beat me into submission, and I settled. Once I gathered myself, that same year my income tripled from the previous year. I decided to swallow my pride and be the man she knew I could be. Can I be brutally honest? Once I started functioning at another level, I liked it and I liked myself better.

Nicole was my pusher, her life can be summed up in three words, Class, Style and Excellence. She not only pushed me, but she also pushed everyone that came into her presence.

When you surround yourself with people of that caliber, your life will never be the same. Starting now, your inner circle is about to change.

At New Community the church, the ministry I pastor, we take seriously the idea of not surrounding ourselves with BO BOs, Bo Bo is a fictitious person, that person wants nothing and doesn't want to be anything.

Are you ready to explore the three people you need in your life?

THE PUSHER

The pusher is a unique person, they will move you beyond your comfort zone. The pusher is not concerned about your attitude or feelings.

The pusher is like a good parent, they are more concerned about the final results and not being your friend. I have discovered that weak people surround themselves with people that will entertain their unwillingness to grow and become the person God ordained them to be.

The Pusher has one job, "to make you uncomfortable." People grow when they are willing to operate in an environment that makes them uncomfortable. The discomfort creates a drive and desire to move beyond the normal. When you finally experience the new normal of success you will never want to go back.

If you operate in immaturity, you will reject the pusher and run back to the safe zone. The safe zone is the worst place to be in your life. In the safe zone there is no growth or expansion. As a matter of fact the safe zone will allow you to be the same and never pass judgment on you.

That comfort is only good for a season,

life will pass you by and you wonder why other people are living your dream. I got tired of people living my dream. I became serious about not being the smartest person in the room. I found people that made me feel stupid, not condescending but intelligent in things beyond my comprehension. I decided not to be intimidated by them, but to extract from them what I needed.

Kinda like a tick, I attach myself to them to draw from them what I need to grow. People of great influence, produce so much you can never exhaust their ability to inspire.

Can I share a secret with you?

Your pusher is probably already in your life. They are waiting for you to ask them to push you. Remember you need to be humble and recognize you need the push. I have discovered people love you, but will leave you spiritually, emotionally, intellectually bankrupt until you allow them to help you.

Most people are too fragile to hear the truth and be pushed to greatness.

Follow these steps as you discover your pusher.

1. Be willing to submit.
2. Be willing to be uncomfortable.
3. Be willing to try something new.
4. Be willing to fail.
5. Be willing to grow.
6. Be willing to move beyond familiar.

CERTIFICATE TO GROW

I hereby humbly submit myself to your leadership and guidance to become a better version of myself.

_____

Your Name

_____

Pusher Name

THE COACH

Michael Jordan hands down was the greatest basketball player to ever live. There are many talented players that need a Phil Jackson in your life. The coach will put you in the right position.

Not only did Phil Jackson bring out the best in Jordan, he did the same for Kobe and Shaq. The coach understands that you are talented but they are not intimidated to the point they don't tell you the truth.

Business people hire coaches to make them successful, but the coach can only work with your willingness to submit.

You may not have the talent of Jordan or Kobe but you do have the God given ability to make a difference in the earth.

Let's start there, what are you called to do?

_____

_____

_____

Once you understand your calling something happens on the inside. Ok, you might not know your calling or you are afraid to share what it is. Most people are stuck, they have accepted what life has presented to them and they decide to settle.

What areas in your life have you settled?

_____

_____

_____

Your coach will get you in position to succeed. Your coach has one goal in mind, getting you to the championship.

Yes, talent is good, but discipline and consistency will bring out the best in your life. Watch this, a good coach will ignore what you say and stick to the game plan.

Most people don't have a game plan. The old saying still holds true, "*Most people don't plan to fail, they fail to plan*".

If you are going to live in your future, you may as well plan for it. A good coach will make planning a priority.

"The more time you spend contemplating what you should have done...you lose valuable time planning what you can and will do." – Lil Wayne

Every good coach has a game plan and it's up to the players to execute. The debate still lingers in the NFL, was it Bill Belichick or Tom Brady?

I have come to the realization that it was a little bit of both. Tom Brady left the New England Patriots after 20 successful seasons, to start a new era with the Tampa Bay Buccaneers and won a Super Bowl. I believe if he stayed in New England he probably could have won at least one or two more in New England.

A good coach creates an environment that allows success to happen for all parties. I have another example of a coach/player duo. Andy Reid took a chance on Patrick Mahomes, he saw something special in the quarterback from Texas Tech.

On the eve of Super Bowl 57, people are debating, is it Patrick Mahomes or Andy Reid? Together, they are winning super bowls and creating history. Does it really matter if a good coach and talent wins championships?

I think about the Dallas Cowboys, when they won those championships, Tom Landry and Barry Switzer had the authority to make those crucial decisions. Chuck Noll and the Pittsburgh steelers made beautiful music together. The coach in your life must be given the authority to be direct and make decisions that win championships. I will not mention Jerry Jones and his wanting to be the coach and the owner. LOL

The coach has value beyond the game, for example my high football Coach Joe Buggs and his wife Loretta are still part of my life, I was last coached by him over 40 years ago. A good coach will not only teach you the game, but they will also teach you life.

How do you find the coach?

They are probably in your life already. What is it that you want to do? Find that person who understands the ins and outs of your dream. Find a person that is doing what you want to do at a high level.

Please understand your coach, may never be your buddy. You may never eat dinner with them or hang out with them. Be a student and learn to extract all the things you need to grow. Learn the playbook for what you are trying to do and become.

When you walk closely to a person, you pick up small things they do. You learn positive habits and you begin to erase self-destructive behavior and understanding. Most people don't know what they don't know.

Your coach will push you to be uncomfortable. Did you notice your coach will push you to be the greatest? The difference between the coach and pusher, the coach is in the game with you. When you are traveling the road of unknown, it is important to know that they have been where you are going.

A good coach is a student of the game. They understand the play, therefore they can teach it with confidence and conviction.

Let's not make coaching about sports only, in a good home parents are often the first coach their children will ever see. Parents teach their children the game of life, if they understand it themselves.

In business, there are coaches, every good president or CEO serves as good for that organization. Everything in life rises and falls on leadership.

The coach should never solicit direction from the subordinates; he doesn't always drive the bus, but surely he understands the route the bus must take to get to its proper destination.

Stop looking for people that agree with you, but find those who are willing to challenge you and bring out the best in you. Find the dog on the inside and become what you are destined to be.

You are only one coach away from becoming what you know you should be.

I see that smile on the inside, right now something is brewing on the inside. You haven't had that feeling in a long time.

That's the beast inside waiting to be unleashed into the world. You can do it!!!!!

The key to finding a good coach is: Ask yourself the below questions, it will make a difference when you find your coach.

1. Do they have Competency?
2. Do they have Conviction?
3. Do they have Consistency?
4. Do they have Credibility?
5. Do they have Courage to Challenge you?

CERTIFICATE TO GROW

I hereby humbly submit myself to your leadership and guidance to become a better version of myself.

_____

Your Name

_____

Coach Name

THE INSTRUCTOR

You are almost there, you got an understanding on the pusher, the coach and now let's stretch and understand the instructor.

I have a question for you, are you a good student? Whether your answer is yes or no, write a response, this will help you grow.

_____

_____

The best way to describe the instructor, most people don't know what they don't know.

The instructor is a very special person we need in our lives. The instructor helps erase ignorance.

"Birds of a feather flock together."

Without knowing much about you, I can say most of your friends have similar lifestyles, habits and opinions comparable to you. At my church I made a bold statement, I said don't tell me about you, let me talk to the people you talk to often and it will paint a clear picture of who you are.

Unfortunately, people seldom stretch beyond the circle of influence.

The instructor exposes you to more.

Yes exposure erases ignorance and gives you a different perspective on life. I remember the first time I traveled to Europe with my darling wife Nicole who passed on January 24, 2024 from Ovarian cancer.

Together we desired to venture beyond the areas that we grew up in. I am sick of people getting offended when we talk about living beyond the borders that we grew up in.

Nicole and I understand the importance of getting instructions about the things that were foreign to what we know. We cherished the instructions from people greater than us.

Those life lessons allowed us to grow and become the people we are.

Instruction is not only about exposure, it forces you to yearn for a different environment. The environment creates an atmosphere conducive to learning and growing.

Remember I said the instructor teaches you what you don't know. The instructor can be a person, more often than not instructions come from the desire to want to be better.

When you hunger and thirst for growth you begin to extract information from every part of your life. Mistakes can teach you so much about life. Some of the greatest lessons learned are from mistakes. Most people don't learn from mistakes, why they spend too much time in denial or trying to be perfect. I don't mind admitting when I am wrong or made an error.

Once you come to the realization that you were wrong, growth takes place.

Growth is the result of understanding where you missed and the determination not to go that route again.

How do you find an instructor? Most instructors are not at an institution of higher learning. You must know what you want. Knowing what you want in life is instrumental in finding that instructor for that phase of life.

I have multiple instructors, they are designed to help me become a better person, they are different from the coach and the pusher.

Many instructors I have in my life don't even know my name. Remember what I said earlier, the pusher, the coach and the instructor don't have to be your BFF, they play a specific role to help you grow and become a better version of yourself.

The instructor will expose you to what you didn't know that you didn't know. Are they people that you get around to help you begin to feel bigger, better, stronger and smarter.

Guess what, you just found your instructor. A good student will take notes and cherish the information they get from the instructor.

For most people, if you are a person of faith your pastor can be an instructor in your life. Pick a ministry that does more than make you feel good, you need a church that will challenge you spiritually, mentally, socially, financially and so on.

When your pastor speaks revelation, it is designed to erase ignorance in your life. When you get instruction, you are now accountable to do better and be better.

What are some areas you need clarity and instruction in?

_____

_____

_____

Another instructor you may have are people you don't know personally but who consistently give life changing information. Social media has changed the game, you can subscribe to a podcast and get consistent information and teaching from them. One of my mentors, Eric Thomas, I listen to his podcast at least four hours a week. This information has changed my thinking and outlook in life. Remember your instructor doesn't have to know your name.

Another instructor could be your parents or a close relative or friend. If they are successful at something, don't ask questions, just watch what they do. The greatest lesson is watching what people do. In the past I was consumed too much by what people were saying versus watching what they did.

When I started looking at the actions of people it made all the difference.

Actions always point you to the truth. Be careful not to get intoxicated by the words people speak. You should always watch what people do. Actions are indicators and what people believe.

Yes, words have power but they can be deceiving.

Side bar, Have you read my book called "The Power of Words" if not please get you a copy.

Ok. Let's summarize the potential instructors. You have to get this write finding quality instructors will raise your life to another level quickly.

Bishop Rosie S. O'neal would often say, the difference between you this year and next year are two things.

"The books you read and the people you associate with."I took that statement literally, I have surrounded myself with instructors that help me erase ignorance on a consistent basis.

Most people only strive for learning more, part of my growth is my willingness to erase ignorance, that only happens through quality instruction. I am committed to being a student the rest of my life.

Your Instructor Could Be:

1. Your Pastor
2. Your Social Media Personality
3. Your Friends
4. Your Parents

CERTIFICATE TO GROW

I hereby humbly submit myself to your leadership and guidance to become a better version of myself.

_____

Your Name

_____

Instructor Name

In conclusion, the better you are is just a few adjustments away. One scripture I used in the past to transform my life is Romans 12:2 Amplified Bible

And do not be conformed to this world [any longer with its superficial values and customs], but be transformed and progressively changed [as you mature spiritually] by the renewing of your mind [focusing on godly values and ethical attitudes], so that you may prove [for yourselves] what the will of God is, that which is good and acceptable and perfect [in His plan and purpose for you].

The ultimate goal is to be the best version of yourself, those 3 people's lives have limited influence. You must still do the work.

You can do it, I know you can.

Pastor Anthony
Remember, we are Powered by A.I.
(Anthony Inspiration)